And then the sun comes out again.
It is hot.

The snow is white and crisp. Our hands are cold when we build a snowman.

The wind stops. But the sky is grey, and the snow comes.

The wind begins to blow.

We put on coats and boots to keep us warm and dry. And we need to take the washing in before it gets wet.

But look! Clouds are covering the sun.
It is starting to rain.

It is hot.
Let's go for a swim to cool off.

My Book Of
WEATHER

Anthony Lewis

LEOPARD

For Frank

First published in 1996 by Leopard Books,
a division of Random House UK Ltd,
20 Vauxhall Bridge Road, London SW1V 2SA

© 1996 Anthony Lewis

ISBN 0 7529 0173 7

Printed in Singapore